THE CHEMO
DIARIES

CARRIE KULIEV

ISBN: 978-1-4669-4806-8 (sc)
ISBN: 978-1-4669-4805-1 (e)

Trafford rev. 07/21/2012

 www.trafford.com

North America & international
toll-free: 1 888 232 4444 (USA & Canada)
phone: 250 383 6864 ♦ fax: 812 355 4082

CONTENTS

2. Remission—Part I

3. Cancer—Part II

4. Remission—Part II

TO J.T. AND MAX

The light of my life and joy of my heart

TO MY PRAYER PARTNERS

Like Jesus you are

CANCER—PART I

INTRODUCTION

On 12/30/07 I felt a lump on my left collar bone. I was a little concerned and that night during my devotions I read these verses "And when this mortal has put on immortality, then shall the written word be fulfilled, "Death is swallowed up in victory. Death, where is your victory? Death where is your sting?" I Corinthians 15: 54-55. I found comfort in these verses, but there was a part of me that went "Yikes!"

1/3/08 I went to the doctor's and was immediately asked if cancer ran in my family.

This book comprises the letters to my prayer partners. I already had been in contact with them to pray for the marriage counseling I was going through with my husband who had left me two years previously. That was an enormous "valley" in my life, but I am continually amazed at the strength, love, lessons and even joy that can be found in the valleys.

CARRIE'S NEW REQUEST

1/4/08

Hi everyone!

Well, since I have you all set up on my nifty computer as prayer partners, I'm going to throw another request at you. I have two lumps on my lymph nodes and something in my chest (info. thanks to a CT scan I had yesterday). I am going in for outpatient surgery Monday or Tuesday to get a biopsy. I think the prayer request is obvious—"Hey, where did those lumps go? Hum, nothing here but a healthy body." We'll see. I'll be sure to keep you posted as soon as I know anything!

God bless you, guys!! I love you!!

Carrie

He who believes in me will live . . . and . . . will never die.
John 11: 25-26

That's a beautiful thing!

THE DIAGNOSIS

1/9/08

Howdy!

Well, it's Hodgkin's Lymphoma. Which, I want to point out, is one of the more curable forms of cancer. So the new prayer request is that it is in an early stage. I'll be finding out soon as well as starting on chemotherapy in the next few days. Tomorrow I have a PET scan, and I'll be meeting with the oncologist soon. Fun, fun, fun!!

I must say, your prayers are being answered. I feel little to no anxiety (it's that peace that surpasses all understanding). Pray for J.T. and Max as they get to face more "stuff" in their lives. Also, for my parents who have been an ENORMOUS help!

Thank you, dear friends, for your prayers!!

Blessings,
Carrie

Don't worry about anything;
Instead, pray about everything.
Tell God what you need,
And thank him for all he has done.
If you do this, you will experience God's peace . . .
Philippians 4: 6-7

ANOTHER REQUEST

1/13/08

Hello everyone!!

I can't express how overwhelmed I am by your love and support. You all are amazing!!

I met with the oncologist on Friday and I really liked him. He was very up front with how I will be feeling for the next six months. Basically, he said to just write off 2008. However, he also said next year I will be healthy, my hair will be growing back, and I will have a new appreciation of life. Gotta love that!!

I am going in for a bone marrow biopsy on Tuesday, and on Wednesday the doctor will tell me what stage my cancer is in. I will probably be starting chemotherapy next week.

I will keep you informed as to how I'm doing. Again, I am overwhelmed by your prayers and support!! I dearly love you guys!!

Love and blessings,
Carrie

Those who live in the shelter of the Most High
will find rest in the shadow of the Almighty.
This I declare of the Lord:
He alone is my refuge, my place of safety;
He is my God, and I am trusting Him.

Psalm 90:1-2

GOOD NEWS

1/16/08

Hi Everyone!!

Thank you, thank you for your prayers! My cancer is in stage 2 (better than 3 or 4), and I may only have to do chemotherapy as opposed to chemo **and** radiation therapy. Wohoo!!

I start chemo next Tuesday, and I'll be going in for a treatment every other week. This is wonderful considering I feel like I've been living in doctor's offices the past three weeks.

So it's all good news! By the way, does anyone have any cute hats collecting dust in their closets?

I'll write more later. I'm beat! This mental stuff is exhausting!!

I am filled with an overwhelming sense of gratitude to God and you for all this love and support!!

Much Love and Blessings,
Carrie

For he will rescue you from every trap
And protect you from the fatal plague.
He will shield you with his wings.
He will shelter you with his feathers.
His faithful promises are your armor and protection.

Psalms 90:3-4

CARRIE'S PROGRESS

1/26/08

Okay, people! I always thought the phrase "the medicine is worse than the disease" was referring to Milk of Magnesia. I may have mentioned earlier that the doctor said I may not need the full 6 months of chemo. At the time I thought, "That's nice." You can now find me on my knees pleading, "PLEEEEEASE Lord, let this be less than 6 months!" If you follow my example, I would be eternally grateful.

Yeah! Wow! Words cannot explain it. I was happy to get vertical to write this email. Thankfully, they said the very first week would be the worst (and that would be me trying to stay positive). I really cannot thank you ENOUGH for your prayers!! The Lord, you guys, and all of your support are what is going to get me through this. God bless you!!!! I'll write more, when I'm up and around (let's hope that's not August).

I love you all very much!!!
Carrie

Do not be afraid of the terrors of the night,
Nor fear the dangers of the day,
Nor dread the plague that stalks in darkness,
Nor the disaster that strikes at midday.

Psalms 90: 5-6

MORE REQUESTS

1/27/08

I just want to say that you all are terrific! Your prayers are being heard! I actually ate some normal food today and almost wept with joy! After six months, I'll be coming out with a book on the 5 million ways to prepare jello and oatmeal.

I just want to throw out a prayer request for my son, Max, who is sick with pneumonia. When you're on chemo, you can't be near a germ (your immune system is at its most pitiful). So, I will be at one end of the house, Max will be at the other and my parents (God bless them) will be waiting on us and getting us to doctor's appointments. Please pray for strength for my parents, and that Max and I will feel better quickly this week.

Thank you, thank you!! I'll be in touch!

Much, much love,
Carrie

If you make the Lord your refuge,
If you make the Most High your shelter,
No evil will conquer you;
No plague will come near your dwelling.
For he orders his angels
to protect you wherever you go.
They will hold you with their hands
to keep you from striking your foot on a stone.

Psalm 90: 9-12

CHOCOLATE ANYONE?

1/30/08

Hi Everyone!

I feel like a human again! Yay!! I have a feeling my life is going to be one week bad—one week better for a while. I am grateful for the one week better. Next Tuesday I go in for my next chemo treatment, and they are going to try a different anti-nausea "cocktail" in hopes that my bad week improves. Thank you for your prayers, and don't forget those "less than 6 months of chemo" prayers!!

I went to the radiation therapist today. I'm guessing nobody likes going to get radiation, because they put boxes of chocolate and peanut M & M's in the waiting room to get you there. Works for me! Anyway, I am going to need radiation. The tumor in my chest was big enough that there is concern that it may come back. Radiation should prevent this. So bring on the radiation and the chocolates. They do the radiation for 4 weeks after chemo is completely done. Well, I sure am looking forward to 2009. How about you? I'm beginning to understand that "new appreciation of life" I am going to feel.

Max looks better. The color is back in his cheeks. Thank you so much for praying for him and my parents (God bless them).

Love and Blessings,
The Human Carrie

The Lord says, "I will rescue those who love me.
I will protect those who trust in my name.
When they call on me, I will answer;
I will be with them in trouble.
I will rescue them and honor them.
I will satisfy them with a long life
And give them my salvation.

Psalm 90: 14-16

COMA ANYONE?

2/10/08

I will give a big reward to the person who can put me in a coma for the first four days after chemo. My goodness! Apparently, we have not come up with the best anti-nausea cocktail for me yet. "Yet" being the key word here. It gives me hope.

I'm feeling MUCH better today! Hallelujah! New things in my life include giving myself shots (because my white blood cell count is so low). It's hard to surprise yourself with a needle like the nurses do. Also, a dear friend is shaving my head today. My dog, Hobbes (a red golden retriever), is having sympathy hair loss with me, so between the two of us we are all swimming in red hair over here. Ick! Time to go, hair!

Fun, fun, fun! Actually, I am so looking forward to this up-coming week as a human being again! I don't know how I am voluntarily going to enter that chemo room again. This too shall pass—thank heavens!

Wow! Your prayers, love and support are carrying me through this! I can't thank you enough!! Again, please pray for my dear parents and J.T. & Max. Also, that most important of prayers (okay, so my priorities are a bit mixed up) that I only have four more treatments of chemo to go.

Much, much love,
Carrie

O Lord, hear me as I pray;
Pay attention to my groaning . . .
Because of Your unfailing love,
I can enter Your house . . .

Psalm 5:1,7

BALD IS BEAUTIFUL

2/12/08

Top Ten reasons I love having no hair!

#10—"Hat hair" a thing of the past.

#9—A hurricane cannot mess up hair do.

#8—If I get drafted, I already have the hair cut.

#7—No checking the mirror to see if hair is okay (in fact, you tend to avoid mirrors altogether).

#6—Save electricity (no blow dryers, curling irons).

#5—No gel, no mousse, no hairspray.

#4—No guilt over not knowing how to properly apply gel, mousse and hairspray.

#3—"Lather, rinse, repeat" all history.

#2—No guilt over not "repeating".

And the #1 reason I love having no hair—No bad hair days!! Wohoo!!

It's all wonderful until one of your children looks at you and says, "AGH! Mom, put on a hat!"

Oh well, in the meantime, I'll just enjoy the ride. And be forever envious of bald men!

I love you, guys!!

Love and Blessings,
Carrie

BEWARE OF DOCTORS
WITH CHOCOLATE

2/19/08

Hi everyone!!

Well, in a couple of hours I'm off to chemo session number three. Some of you have never seen a chemo room, so let me describe it for you. It is a large room filled with lounge chairs and smiling nurses. They put up your feet, give you pillows & blankets and a stack of magazines. It is a completely cushy experience. There is even a table with coffee, tea and Uh Oh! Warning—Warning—a large tray filled with chocolate. Beware of the doctors and nurses that feel so bad for you that they offer you chocolate!! I find it no small coincidence that the only chocolate I've seen in a doctor's office are in chemo and radiation rooms. Maybe I'll find more chocolate once I've had a stroke or heart attack. We'll see.

Anyway, we're trying some new things this week in the area of my plethora of prescription drugs. I'm maxed out on my anti-nausea drugs, so we're adding steroids (maybe I can now bench press more than 5 pounds) and a tranquilizer (Hey, I DID want to be in a coma for 4 days—maybe I'll get my wish). The "fun" starts about an hour after chemo, and just knowing you guys are praying for me can take me from the deepest depths to cloud nine pretty quick. You are all the best part of this whole experience! I thank you a million times over!!

God bless you, guys! He is blessing me enormously through this!! Talk to you soon!!

Much Love,
Carrie—the soon-to-be spaced out blob

Don't be afraid,
for I am with you.
Do not be dismayed,
for I am your God.
I will strengthen you.
I will help you.
I will uphold you
with my victorious right hand.

Isaiah 41:10

SHOPPING THERAPY—
WORKS FOR ME!

2/26/08

Hi everyone!

Oh boy! Carrie's ability to maintain a cheerful attitude is dwindling. It's still in there somewhere-just dwindling. I spent all day Sunday in the ER. I was extremely dizzy, and it turns out I was dehydrated. I spent so much time in a stupor last week, I guess I forgot to drink enough. I, personally, think I have the perfect POW torture routine—give someone chemo and then tell them they have to drink 10 glasses of fluid each day. I can't express how horrible ANY liquid looks when you're this nauseous. So, pray I can force the fluids in me next week.

I just got back from the doctor's office. The nurse could tell I was a little down, and she went on to tell me that this chemo I'm dealing with is the worst of the worst. They're hitting me with the killer stuff, I have the killer nausea, and I have every right to be a bit depressed. It's weird that that made me feel better, but it did. She also told me to go out and spend some money this week-end. If I get out this week-end, I'll be happy. If I'm feeling really good, I'll be sure to have my VISA card in tow.

Okay, enough complaining! God is good!! He's teaching me so much, and touching my heart with His Word every time I read it—it's blowing me away!! And you guys!! Your prayers, gifts, cards, emails!! You are blowing me away just as much!! How can I thank you?!?

After my next chemo, they are going to take a PET scan. This will decide how much longer I'll need the chemo treatments. I'll be sure to let you know when that is. The prayer is "a cancer free scan". If it is, I'll have two more chemos and then radiation. We won't even discuss what it will be if it's not cancer free. The Lord knows I'm pretty maxed out on the ol' character building experiences. We'll see—He's in charge.

God bless you guys!!

Much, much love,
Carrie

I am sick at heart.
How long, O Lord until you restore me?
Return, O Lord, and rescue me.
Save me because of your unfailing love.

Psalm 6: 3-4

TATTOOS AND MARIJUANA

2/28/08

I was innocently watching an episode of "CSI-Miami" when one of the characters got caught purchasing marijuana for his sister. She was using it to help her with her chemotherapy nausea. Then a friend of mine was innocently watching "Desperate Housewives", and one of the characters got her only relief from chemo nausea from some marijuana laced brownies. So you can imagine how my ears perked up when the hot topic in the chemo room among the patients was "Does marijuana really help this dreadful nausea?" The nurses, I think, have been asked this a million times, and the answer is "If you have not used marijuana in the past, it ain't gonna help you now." Lord help me, but I was seriously considering having the Christian Women's Guild score me some pot!

It turns out, I get to have three tattoos. One for each tumor. They will be used to help zap me for my radiation. I have requested a cross, a heart and a butterfly, but have a feeling I am only going to get "X marks the spot".

The lesson here: "Never say never?" I really wanted to let you know I'm feeling MUCH better today. My sense of humor is back—as warped as it may be. A dear friend is taking me out to Palm Desert this week-end. Nothing like a little warm, dry air to lift the spirits!

I love you, guys!!

In Him,
Carrie

I will lift up my eyes to the mountains (surrounding Palm Desert);
From whence shall my help come?
My help comes from the Lord,
Who made heaven and earth.

Psalm 121: 1&2

THE SEA OF DESPAIR

3/6/08

Hello Everyone!

I told a friend that getting ready for chemo is like preparing for a trip. You do the laundry, buy extra groceries. Alas, it is a trip to the Sea of Despair. My postcards would read something like "Having a miserable time, glad you're not here. Will be back in a week." The Sea isn't utterly horrible. There are always plenty of things one can learn there. And there's just nothing like being lifted up by the prayers and support of your loved ones! So, thank you for getting me through the Sea.

I just wanted to let you know that I will be having my PET scan and CT scan on Monday at 9:00 am. I have a doctor's appt. on Tuesday at 4:00 pm, and the doc said he should have the results by then. "Please, Lord, please let the cancer be gone!" That will be my prayer, please feel free to copy me. I'll be checking knees for calluses. Just kidding!! I will be sure to let you know what happens as soon as I do!

I love you, guys!! Thank you so much for everything!!

Love and blessings,
Carrie

Trust me in your times of trouble,
And I will rescue you,
And you will give me glory.

Psalm 50:15

GOOD NEWS & AN IMPORTANT ARCHAEOLOGICAL FIND

3/11/08

Thank you, Lord!!! The PET scan was clean, and the CT scan showed three shrinking tumors. The doctor said that was exactly what they were hoping for! Wohoo!! I will have 2 to 4 more chemo treatments—pray for 2—these treatments are making me MENTAL! After that I'll have my four weeks of radiation. The end is coming within viewing range. Again, I would have had no hope of surviving this illness (and its cure) without you!!!!

An important archaeological find was made by myself yesterday. I discovered the exact location of hell. It's in Irvine, CA (where I got my scans). If you happen to visit there and they offer you an "Apple Smoothie" (contrast for the CT scan), you need to say "Get thee behind me Satan!" The experience was highlighted by me having to lie perfectly still for one hour (the PET scan), while mentally challenging myself to not lose my drink lest I have to force it down again. I think you can name an archaeological find after yourself, so let's call it "Carrie's Personal Hell". I'll let you know when I have to go back there, so you can pray that "Apple Smoothie" is not on the menu.

THE TIME FRAME

3/18/08

Well, Carrie had quite a scare today.

Let me preface that with—each chemo treatment is two parts taken at different times. For example, I have gone in for treatment 1A, 1B, 2A & 2B. These have taken me eight weeks to accomplish. So at some point I realized, and the nurse confirmed, that when the doctor said 2-4 treatments he actually meant 4-8 more times in the chemo room for me. Oh horrors!! Soooo when I asked the doctor how many treatments I had left, I was afraid to hear the answer. "We're going to go with 2 more treatments!" Thank you, God!!!

But it all goes to show—it's all perspective, isn't it? I wanted nothing more than one more time at chemo, and now three more times is looking pretty good!!

It's also nice to have a time line to go by. It's looking like chemo will be finished at the end of April, and radiation should finish just before the boys get out of school for the summer.

Again, thank you for your prayers!! It never ceases to amaze me how gross one can feel. It looks like I have squillions of funny emails from you guys! I'm going to savor them one by one!! You're the best!!

Much love and blessings,
Carrie

The Lord will work out his plans for my life—
For your faithful love, O Lord, endures forever.
Don't abandon me, for you made me.

Psalm 138: 8

ATTACK OF THE KILLER FATIGUE

3/29/08

Someone throw Carrie a rope . . . she's drowning in the Sea! I asked the doc if it was normal that I now had no more "good" days, and unfortunately, he said yes. I guess this stuff builds up in your system, and it has attacked me as the killer fatigue. I have morphed from the Creature of the Black Lagoon to The Blob. Not having the strength to hold one's head up for two weeks solid is a whole new experience for me. I may have 6 more weeks of it to look forward to, but then I have to remind myself that I am being spared 8 additional weeks after that. Thank heavens!!

So it's 5 down and 3 to go. I truly would not be making it without the visitations, phone calls, and emails. Distraction is the key to survival at this point. You're all doing a great job! Keep it coming!!!

Things to be thankful for:

I just had my teeth cleaned and had no cavities. I know I sound like a kid, but the amount of things that can go wrong with your mouth and teeth while on chemo is enormous (teeth dying, horrible mouth sores, etc.) So that's a beautiful thing.

I have sure enjoyed connecting and reconnecting with all of you!!

I still love having no hair. I'm hoping bald comes in style for women!!

J.T. and Max are doing great!! J.T. is on the boys Volleyball Team and is loving it!! They are both enjoying school! They both were a big help to me during their Easter Break!!

I just can't thank you enough, yet again!! Pray me through the month of April!!

I love you!!
Carrie

Keep on praying. No matter what happens, always be thankful, For this is God's will for you who belong to Christ Jesus.

I Thessalonians 5: 17-18

NO CHEMO TODAY

4/1/08

Hi Everyone!

I sure am looking forward to the day when I can make your prayer lives a little LESS active! Well, I wasn't out of it last week for nothing. I am definitely fighting something. Unfortunately, we're still trying to figure out what's going on. This cough I've had for a month is now making it hard for me to breathe. Yeah, that's fun! The pulmonary doctor set up an appt. for me on Friday. I'll never survive that long! I may be going into the ER tomorrow if I can't move up that appt. I did get a chest x-ray which showed nothing, except that the tumors are shrinking—so that's good news!

I'm also fighting fevers and chills. I'm a most pitiful creature over here!! It could be an infection, allergic reaction, or one of the chemo drugs can cause this. I thank you for your prayers! Pray this all results in a nice deep breath without coughing soon!! Ahhh! That would be wonderful!

Thanks, my dear friends!! I'll keep you posted!

Much Love and Blessings,
Carrie

The Lord is close to all who call on him,
Yes, to all who call on him sincerely.

Psalm 145:18

The following is from a dear friend who informed my prayer partners what was going on with me

CARRIE'S UPDATE

4/4/08

Hi Everyone,

For those of you who do not know, our dear friend Carrie has been in Mission Hospital since Tuesday, when she took herself to the ER after being unable to breathe and uncontrollable coughing.

I am a little apprehensive to say exactly what the prognosis is, as it has changed and we are waiting for results from a procedure done yesterday morning. However, they did say she had pneumonia and then changed it to a possible allergic reaction to the chemo drugs, so once we know for sure, I will let you all know.

Having said all this, Carrie's parents are unable to be with her this weekend, and we are looking for some of you great friends who would like to bless her and go to the hospital and spend some time with her. If you can only spare 30-60 minutes with her I know that she would greatly appreciate it.

I have Saturday covered and am looking for people to go and spend some time with her on Sunday, if you are able to do that, please let me now ASAP with the time and period of time you are able to be with her. Please do not send or take any flowers or fruit to her, as they are not allowing them in her room.

I know that she would love to see you and please keep her in your prayers!

Love and Blessings,
Caroline

HERE'S TO NEW EXPERIENCES

4/8/08

I'm HOOOOME! Oh, just to walk to my bathroom not attached to a million tubes is WONDERFUL! I got home yesterday afternoon, and was dying to see my emails, but opted for a shower and a good night sleep. I'm happy to report I got both!

Forget the appreciation of life—I now have the appreciation of breathing! Turns out Bleomycin (a chemo drug) and Carrie need to end their friendship. Thankfully, the drug has done its job, and I do not need any more of it! Thank you, God!! This allergic reaction is not completely uncommon—hits about 5% who use it. My poor lungs were infected and inflamed—I'm now on quite the antibiotic regimen for a couple of weeks!

I learned some new torture techniques for my POW camp. Like when my fever spiked and they packed me in ice—that was fun! And there's always the 6 inch Q-tip down the nose—OHHH YEAH. And a sure fire confession grabber would be the three meals a day with cling peaches, mystery meat, and rice that tastes like dirt. "I defect! I will tell you everything!"

I must say, I got in the wrong line of work. If you want to work with the nicest people in the world, get on the hospital staff at Mission Hospital. I met gazillions of people—ALL of them beyond a blessing! I was amazed!! Even the nurse with the 6 inch Q-tip said, "This is nothing personal." I should have run for the door!

Hey, you guys!! You all went above and beyond the call of duty helping me recover!! I had so many visitors on Saturday and Sunday—it was great!! I was completely pumped up on steroids, so I was really enjoying myself! (I hate to say I have a new empathy for baseball players). Your prayers, your phone calls, your emails . . . . You all know how to make a girl feel loved!! Everyone of you—like Jesus you are!!

Well, next Tuesday it's back to chemo. Apparently, there's no harm in me skipping these two weeks, so that's good!! Chemo may be looking pretty good after this experience! We'll see!!

I love you, guys!!! Talk to you soon!!! And, Auntie Em, there's no place like home!!

Love and Blessings,
Carrie

Do not be afraid, for I have ransomed you.
I have called you by name; you are mine.
When you go through deep waters and great trouble,
I will be with you.
When you go through rivers of difficulty, you will not drown.
Isaiah 43:1-2

THREE TO GO

4/15/08

I think I said "3 to go" about a month ago. As you may recall, I was drowning in the middle of the Sea of Despair. Thankfully, through your prayers and support, the Mission Hospital staff was able to rescue me. I can now say "three to go" with confidence, and the feeling that wallowing in the shallows of the Sea will not seem nearly so bad. So today I go in for chemo # 6 without the chemo drug I'm deathly allergic to. That's got to be better!!

Again, your prayers are precious!! I can't thank you enough! I'll be in touch—I'll write you from the seaside.

Much Love and Blessings,
Carrie

For God has said,
"I will never fail you
I will never forsake you."
That is why we can say with confidence,
"The Lord is my helper,
so I will not be afraid."

Hebrews 13:5-6

TWO TO GO

4/23/08

Two to go! Two to go! This is my chant! I walk around the house like a monk—chanting. I would like to say the nausea and lack of energy were better, but there is comfort in the fact that in about a month and a half, I should be saying it!!

Keep praying! Everybody's "done" with this illness at this point! It's a true endurance test! I am happy to report that I am breathing well! I will never take oxygen for granted again!!

I love you guys!! Thanks for hanging in there with me!! Two to go! Two to go!

Much Love and Blessings,
Carrie

He alone is my rock
and my salvation,
my fortress where
I will never be shaken.

Psalm 62:2

I SEE THE LIGHT
(AT THE END OF THE TUNNEL)

4/28/08

Hi Everyone!

In 24 hours I'll be able to say "One to go!"

I had a great week-end! I felt energetic and almost back to normal! It was wonderful! Every other week-end I REALLY enjoy food as I never have before. Add that to the list—a new appreciation of FOOD (and, as anyone will confirm, I've always had a pretty healthy appreciation of food).

As I was doing laundry today I realized I have pretty much only worn pajamas and sweats for the past four months. I must say, I am looking forward to wearing things a little less comfortable when this is all over! I'll have a new appreciation of uncomfortable clothes (this is something I have NEVER had).

One thing I do miss, that I've lost recently, is my eye lashes. Hair is one thing—it's easily covered up with a hat or scarf. I feel I have a whole new look without eye lashes. I can see my ad. in "Match.com" now—"If you like the look of a hard boiled egg, then I'm the girl for you!" I guess I'll have to add eye lashes to my list of things I'll appreciate again!

Thank you for praying me through the next few weeks!! We're getting there.

Much Love and Blessings,
Carrie

Be glad
for all God is planning
for you.
Be patient in trouble,
and always be prayerful.

Romans 12:12

A LITTLE POEM

5/2/08

O Nausea, Nausea!
Wherefore art thou Nausea!
Deny thy barfing and refuse thy grossness;
Or, if thou wilt not, be but sworn my enemy,
And I'll keep chanting "One to go!"

from Romeo and Juliet (with paraphrasing)

Thank you for your prayers this week!! I love you, guys!!!
Talk to you soon!!

Much Love and Blessings,
Carrie

LOSING IT

5/7/08

Hi everyone!

Well, I am truly like Pavlov's dog at this point! Yesterday, when I went to my doctor's appt., I just walked past that chemo room and thought I was going to lose my lunch. Just the sight and smell gets me going now. It makes me that much more thankful I just have ONE TO GO!

Thank you for praying for me last week. By Tuesday (one week after chemo) I start wondering if I should start writing my will. Then Wednesday, I start to feel MUCH better, and tomorrow I will feel about a thousand times better than today. So I am very much looking forward to this "good" week-end, and I'll only have one more week-end where I am contemplating my last will and testament. The mental highs and lows are definitely making me loony. Hopefully this is over one step before I enter the funny farm.

Happy Acres is the place for me
Insane living is the life for me
Land spreading out so far and wide
Why are there doctors and nurses where I abide?

I told you. Loony.

I love you, all!! Again, I couldn't have made it without you!!! Almost there!!

God bless you!!

Much Love,
Carrie

Be strong and courageous,
Do not be afraid or terrified . . .
for the Lord your God goes with you;
he will never leave you nor forsake you.

Deuteronomy 31:6

. . . even if you go a bit mental.

LAST ONE

5/12/08

I have a happy story. A friend of mine's mother takes her dog to the hospital once a week to visit the radiation patients to cheer them up. When I asked if she visits the chemo patients, she said, "Oh no! They are way too miserable!" Carrie, with the few brain cells she has left, put together the fact that that means radiation patients are not nearly as miserable as chemo patients! Wohoo!

Actually, I have heard all the stories of radiation patients. From no side effects to not being able to be around family members or touch metal. I guess I will be getting a pretty low dose, and my possible side effects are an esophagus that burns a bit and NAUSEA (my sworn enemy). NO! NO! Anything but that! Needless to say, there's my big prayer request!

I will get a month long break after chemo (to get all my blood counts up) before I start radiation. I can't believe tomorrow is the LAST chemo. (Lord willing for the rest of my life). A couple of weeks from today I'll actually be able to recuperate from all this. A lot to be thankful for!

Timeline:

May 13-19: suicidal
May 20-June 20: euphoric

May 28: Pulmonary Function Test—to see if there was any damage done to my lungs.

June 20-July 20: Radiation

Sometime after radiation: a PET and CT scan to see if they got it all

My prayer requests for this week are that my cancer is gone (and will never come back), and that my lungs survived the dreaded "bleomycin incident" (my hospital stay). You can also throw in no side effects with radiation therapy.

Thank you, you guys! I love you!!! I can't believe we're there! Last one! Tomorrow!

Much Love & Blessings,
Carrie

. . . nothing can ever separate us from his love.
Death can't and life can't . . .
Our fears for today,
our worries about tomorrow . . .

Romans 8:38-39

QUESTIONS?

5/13/08

Hi Everyone!!

Well, Carrie learned the art of NOT asking any questions your last time at chemo.

First question: —When do you think my hair will start growing back?
—About 4-5 weeks. Maybe longer.

Response—Bummer, I was really looking forward to burning my hats. Oh well, bring on the bald summer.

Before this started, I had a port-a-catheter put into my chest, so the chemo meds. could run directly into a major vein. It only bothers me at night, but it's nothing a pillow can't fix.

Second question:—When do I get to have my port removed?
—At least two years.

Response—Bring on the pillows. I won't think about the fact that I might NEED it again.

Third question: —When do I call the radiation doctor?
—First, I want to double check with the people at City of Hope to make sure that

4 cycles (the 8 treatments I've had) is enough, or if you need two more cycles (4 more treatments).

Response—Wh . . . Wh . . . What? They had better not (Okay, so I'm not too good with quick responses).
My Dad's Response—You think things are bad in China right now? (The response I wish I had—thanks Dad!!)

There was a horrible earthquake in China yesterday.

Anyway, as you can see, we have an emergency situation on our hands. Ohhh, please pray that I'm done. The doctor does not realize he took me from celebration mode to dumping me into the Sea of Despair with my feet in cement.

I will let you know the second I find out. Thank you for celebrating, or if we must, swim in the Sea together!!

Much Love and Blessings,
Carrie

We are pressed on every side
by troubles,
but we are not
crushed and broken . . .
but God never abandons us.
We get knocked down,
but we get up again
and keep going.

2 Corinthians 4: 8-9

AT LEAST
NO RADIATION DIARIES

5/15/08

Hi Everyone!

Well, I just heard from the doctor and here's the scoop. He talked to the head honcho, big cheese, leading expert at City of Hope who said if I was HER patient this is what she would do . . . because I was so allergic to the bleomycin (that whole unable-to-breathe incident), she would not have me go through radiation therapy. But if you eliminate that, 4 cycles of chemo may not be enough. So there it is—2 more cycles (4 treatments) of chemo to go for me. So we reset the count down, and gird our loins. As I've already told many of you, between God and your support, I feel I can conquer pretty much anything. You are all amazing!!! How can I thank you?

Keep praying for my parents and J.T. and Max (all my caregivers) who are taking this pretty well! God bless them!

I love you, guys!! Talk to you soon!!

Much, Much Love,
Carrie

Our help is in the name of the Lord,
Who made heaven and earth.

Psalm 124: 8

SOMEONE'S LIVING RIGHT

5/20/08

Hi Everyone!

Well, somebody out there has come up with the ultimate in anti-nausea prayers. I barely had the dreaded sensation last week. It was definitely the best "bad" week I've had to date. I don't doubt it is all your efforts put together, and believe me, it is a wonderful gift. Thank you! Thank you!! Rather than swimming in the Sea of Despair, I was able to pull up a beach chair and just dip my toes in. Wohoo! Pray this keeps up—I will be able to survive this experience if this is what's in store for the next 8 weeks!

I just got back from the doctor's, and apparently, the four extra chemos should work as well as the radiation would have. They just want to make sure (after my bleomycin incident) that they don't do any further damage to my lungs. I'll admit the word "further" had me a bit concerned (just a bit). They'll know for sure after my lung test. I'll let you know when that is. Right now I am breathing fine, and like I said, I have a whole new appreciation of oxygen!!

Love you guys!! Four to go (oh boy!!).

Much Love and Blessings,
Carrie

You saw me before I was born.
Every day of my life was recorded in your book.
Every moment was laid out
before a single day had passed.

Psalm 139:16

CAN'T SEEM TO GET ENOUGH OF THAT MISSION HOSPITAL

5/25/08

Cling peaches, cling peaches, wherefore art thou cling peaches . . .

Yes, Carrie went back into the land of hospital food, and is happy to report she survived it. Last Thursday about noon I started having a pain in my lungs that became unbearable about 5 pm. So with the aid of a dear friend, I went back to that familiar place—ER. It's become a monthly ritual for me. They did all the familiar tests along with a CT scan, and found nothing. The following morning I had a lung scan and heart ultrasound. Bottom line—they found nothing wrong, and do not know WHAT caused it. I could have pulled a muscle near my lungs (is that impressive, or what?), or it just may be the chemo. The two days and two nights (you can figure out how many meals that would be and know my true suffering) I was there, the pain got gradually better, and by Saturday morning was practically non-existent.

Some good news—the CT scan showed all the tumors in my neck are now gone and the one in my chest is still shrinking. Wohoo! I can still get my chemo treatment next Tuesday. Yay—let's get this over with before the cure kills me! And those employees at that hospital still get the "Nicest People in the World" award!

Please pray for it to be about July 20th SOON! Oh, thank you!!! We'll get there!

Much Love,
Carrie

You will keep in perfect peace
all who trust in you,
whose thoughts are fixed
on you!

Isaiah 26:3

REASONS FOR LIVING?

6/3/08

Well, Carrie is attempting to crawl out of the Sea of Despair, and she is looking for her beach chair! Oh, yeah! I am still nauseous! Yuck! Bleack! Ick! Don't ask me why I am a complete barfing blob this time. We'll probably never know. It was a **bad** week, and I'm happy to have it pretty much behind me!

I have whole new *reasons for living* during my bad weeks. One reason is your emails! I love them. A few of you have made it your personal mission to keep me entertained with fun emails. I can't thank you enough. Another reason for living is my television. Yes, that's right, the idiot box! Without it, I am afraid, I would have gone ga-ga a long time ago. I read that in the 1800's if you got really ill, it was suggested that you place a bowl of goldfish in front of you, so you would have something to entertain you all day. Ga-ga-ga. Granted, that would be an improvement over the game shows my generation had to endure as kids. Nevertheless, by mid-July, my brain should pretty much be a complete pile of mush. I will enjoy NOT looking at a television for a very long time!

I hope this finds all of you well, and most of you looking forward to the end of the school year!! Bring on the summer, but more importantly, bring on mid-July (I'm being a little selfish on that one)! Thank you for your prayers! Three (oh, my) to go!

I love you, guys!!
God bless you!!

Carrie

For I can do all things through Christ who strengthens me.
Philippians 4:13

WHAT'S THIS?

6/10/08

Hi Everyone!

As I've already said (a few times now, I think) I sure would hate to have your prayer lives become boring!! Remember my hospital stay a couple of months ago? My lung doctor got some biopsies of my lung, via my nose, while I was there. I'm happy to report that I was unconscious for this event. Welllll, something finally came up in one of those petrie dishes. I deserve a round of congratulations for getting an infectious disease that only 35 people (on record) have gotten EVER. And I think I get a special round for being the ONLY female to ever get it. Thank you, thank you! I'd say it's nice to be special, but I think I've had more than my share of specialness lately. I have mycobacterium szulgai. It's in the tuberculosis family, but is OBVIOUSLY not as contagious. It is treatable, and not life threatening. You treat it with three toxic meds. Wait a minute . . . does this sound like a repeat of January, or what?! Oh my! I have made a conscience decision to not "go there" in my mind until I talk with the infectious disease specialist which will, hopefully, be soon. I will definitely keep you updated on this new development. My prayer request is, of course, that they have made a mistake, and women still do NOT get this disease.

I am currently swimming in the Sea with my new found friends ABC, NBC, CBS, and my latest addiction, HGTV. I am thankful every day for the pretty colors, and people who will talk to me out of that box. Can you tell, Carrie's losing it!

Thank you for your prayers for my parents and my guys, J.T. and Max.

Well, I'm going to tune out for now (the commercials are over—just kidding!) Again, you are all such a blessing!! You are all a huge part of my healing process that I would like to say is ending in July (Oh, would I like to say that). We'll see. The Eternal Diaries? Hmmmm. Carrie, don't go there.

I love you MUCH, and will talk to you soon (when I'm in my beach chair). God bless you, guys!!!

Much Love,
Carrie

No eye has seen,
no ear has heard,
and no mind has imagined
what God has prepared
for those who love him.

I Corinthians 2:9

MYCOBACTERIUM— SHMYCOBACTERIUM

6/21/08

Hi Everyone!

Well, if I have a bit of advice to offer you, it would be that maybe the internet is not the best way to diagnosis your own illnesses or check out your future treatments. I still haven't heard from the infectious disease specialist, so I thought I would go checking out my new illness on the internet. I found a very informative website and learned that I am number 35 with pulmonary mycobacterium szulgai, and I am actually the fourth female to be diagnosed with the disease. I got to read about each case (many of them alcoholics and chain smokers—I swear to you I am not leading some secret lifestyle). And there it was . . . the treatment . . . "We have found successful treatment with 12 to 18 months of chemotherapy." I was instantly on my knees—Oh Lord! PLEASE no! I proceeded to not sleep well for the next couple of nights until I saw my doctor (the oncologist). He also has heard nothing from the elusive specialist, and told me this may be something that I have lived with for a long time, and there's a good chance I may not have to undergo any treatment at all. So I say mycobacterium—shmycobacterium!! It's all one more lesson in taking one day at a time and keeping your eyes on God! I must be hard headed in learning that one, because the intensity of which I have had to come back to it the past few years is unbelievable!!

Thank you so much for your prayers! I had a good round this time! Lots of energy this week! Yeah!! Keep praying! I find the summers just **take** a lot more energy! Thank yooooouuuu! Two (too many) to go!!

Much, Much Love,
Carrie

The Lord is my light and my salvation—
so why should I be afraid?
The Lord protects me from danger—
so why should I tremble?

Psalm 27:1

A SUCCESSFUL MINISTRY

6/29/08

Hello Everyone!

Yeah! Okay! That round was reminiscent of one of my first rounds of chemo. Bleech!! My doctor said, "Six months from now you'll look back at this experience and say it wasn't that bad." I told him that if I do say that, he has my permission to **WHAP** me upside the back of my head! In fact, you all have permission to do the same!

I am impressed with those of you in the hair growth ministry. I should be pretty much bald from my head to my feet, but my hair and eyelashes are actually growing. The peach fuzz on my head is about one inch long now. I was down to about five eyelashes, and now I have a full set growing in. No way this was supposed to happen until about a month after chemo. So good job prayer warriors for hair growth! You truly have a gift, so feel free to expand your prayers to World Hunger and World Peace! I'll be checking the newspapers!

I am SO looking forward to feeling better this week. I still haven't heard from the infectious disease specialist—I'll keep you posted on that one. Again, pray there is nothing to keep you posted on.

Well, again, thank you's are not enough for your prayers and encouragement! I am blessed!! One to go (deja vu)!

I Love You,
Carrie

God is our refuge and strength,
Always ready to help in times of trouble.

Psalm 46:1

SUNDAY'S A COMIN'

7/9/08

A very dear friend took me to my last (yessssss) chemo today. As we were walking out of the chemo room, she looked at my pitiful, barfy face and said the profound words, "Sunday's a comin'!!"

Backstory—I have an OLD Tony Campolo tape titled "Sunday's A Comin'!" He talks about a message his pastor gave at his church on Good Friday. Here is a small excerpt:

"It's Friday—Jesus is on the cross—He's dead—He's gone—He's no more—but that's Friday—Sunday's a comin'! It's Friday—Mary is crying her eyes out, disciples are running in every direction like sheep with out a shepard—no hope in the world—but that's Friday—Sunday's a comin'! It's Friday—Pilate's washing his hands—Pharisees are calling the shots—the Roman soldiers are strutting around with their spears—but that's Friday—Sundays a comin'!! . . ."

It's Tuesday, I'm FEELING like death, and Sunday for me means beginning to feel better, and better, and better, and beginning a whole new life—I am so curious to see what the Lord has in store for me. Sunday's a comin'!

It's a beautiful thing to think of the events of that first Good Friday, and how everyone's tune changed come that next Sunday morning!

Well, pray that was my last chemo **forever**! I just can't thank you all enough!

Faith sees the invisible
Believes the unbelievable
And receives the impossible
Corrie ten Boom

Thank you all for helping me "receive the impossible"!!! I will keep you posted on my upcoming lung tests and if the infectious disease guy ever calls me.

Much, Much Love,
Carrie

In the multitude of my thoughts within me thy comforts delight my soul.

Psalm 94:19

BETTER & BETTER

7/19/08

Hi Everyone!

Every day, in every way, I'm getting better and better!

I can't express the enormous elation at the thought that I do NOT have to go in for chemo on Tuesday! Please do not despair if you ever need chemo. There are many different chemo drugs. Apparently, I had to take four of the worst, my body reacted horribly, AND I ended up being allergic to one of them. My prognosis was so good, I was shocked that this was truly a six month nightmare. I'm thanking God hourly that it is over, and praying earnestly that it's over for life!! Whew!! Again, thank you for pulling me out of that Sea of Despair over and over!!!

A few days before I started chemo, I had to take a series of lung tests. I will be repeating those tests this Wednesday to see if there was any damage done to my lungs. A percentage of chemo patients get lung damage, and as you know, my lungs have been through their share of fun times these past few months. Let's all pray for a miracle—shall we? "The lungs of a teenager!" It could happen—God's in control! I'll let you know the results as soon as I know.

I will also let you know when I will be going in for my scans—sometime in early August. Also, if I ever hear from the elusive infectious disease guy.

I really AM feeling better every day! I guess it takes a couple of months to get rid of all the weird side effects. As long as the nausea is gone, the rest of the side effects can take their sweet time.

Well, dear friends, I'm at a loss for words when it comes to how grateful I am for you all helping me (and my boys and my parents) get through this!!! I sure love you!! God bless you and your families!! I'll be in touch!

Much Love,
Carrie

The unfailing love of the Lord never ends!
By His mercies we have been kept from complete destruction.
Great is His faithfulness;
His mercies begin afresh each day.

Lamentations 3: 22-23

BACK IN

7/23/08

> I keep trying to get out . . . but they keep pulling me back in!
> Michael Corleone

As you know I have been trying to get a hold of the infectious disease specialist for about a month and a half to no avail. My lung doctor picks up the phone and "Viola" he is speaking to him (those doctors have clout!). They decided now that the chemo is done, it's time to get rid of the mycobacterium szulgai. They are putting me on a regimen of pills, blood tests, eye exams, pulmonary function tests, scans, doctor visits . . . I take it all in stride **UNTIL** the doc mentions one of the pills can cause nausea. I will be taking these pills for at least six months, so you can guess what my prayer request is! My prescriptions will be ready to pick up tomorrow, so you'll probably be hearing from me again in a few days. I think it's time I have that 24 hour candlelight vigil!

Well, I just can't get away from these people. The medical beings—they love me!

The results of my lung tests came back. Some were good and some not so good. We'll see if getting rid of the m. szulgai helps.

I think I was put on this earth to keep your prayer lives hopping!! But really—GOD BLESS YOU! Just knowing you are praying for me . . . I feel I can bask in God's peace. It's a beautiful thing!!

Much Love,
Carrie

He who dwells in the shelter of the Most High
will abide in the shadow of the Almighty.

Psalm 91:1

CARRIE REVISITS
ARCHEOLOGICAL FIND

7/29/08

Hi Everyone!!

First off, I do not have anything to report regarding my reaction to the new drugs, because I have not taken any yet. I will be meeting with Dr. Infectious Disease himself next Tuesday, and I'm hoping to be able to put off the pill popping (9 per day) until September (when school starts). We'll see. I'll let you know what he says.

For those of you who do not know my archaeological find . . . . Carrie has discovered the exact location of hell. It is in Irvine, and I get to revisit it on Monday. Ahhh, the wailing and gnashing of teeth!! The water skiing on the Lake of Fire with my trusty asbestos water skis! Actually, this is where I get my scans done, and last time I was there, I almost lost my "apple smoothie" (the contrast for the CT scan) during my PET scan. I'm sorry if this is too much information. That PET scan can give one the heebie jeebies. You have to lie perfectly still for one hour. About half way through I feel like breaking out into the Funky Chicken to the tune of Staying Alive (my new theme song). Wish me luck!! But, most importantly, please pray for the results of these scans! I can't believe I'm actually on the other side of all of this. I'm praying I stay there!! I will surely let you know the results as soon as I do!!

Thank you all for all of your prayers! To feel peace in the middle of all this stuff is truly a miracle!

Much Love,
Carrie

I wait quietly before God,
for my hope is in Him.

Psalm 62:5

REMISSION—PART I

THE OTHER SIDE

8/5/08

Hi Everyone!

Praise God from whom all blessings flow . . . and Carrie has been blessed the past two days!

Thank you, thank you for your prayers for my scans. The experience was MUCH improved thanks to the omission of the chemo nausea!! Whew! What a difference! That smoothie (a banana one this time) is definitely the "highlight" of the whole two hour ordeal. And it's a good thing the PET scan operator announced that there were "only 5 minutes to go", because I could feel those feathers breaking out for my Funky Chicken dance.

Today I met with my Infectious Disease Doctor who turned out to be a very nice person. He answered my squillion questions regarding this disease. I'll try to give you the FAQ answers: You catch it environmentally (water, air, who knows). I am number 11 to have contracted this particular strain (I'm getting more special by the minute). They would not have treated the disease, but they do not want any more damage done to my lungs (caused by the Bleomycin—love that Bleomycin). I will be taking my many pills for 9 to 12 months (that's a lot of pills). The good news—I can start taking these meds. in September, AND if any of them make me feel sick, there are options. Sooo Lord willing, my nauseous days should be close to an end!! Yessssss!

NOW, are you ready to do a dance of your own? I am officially in remission!!! Wooooohooooooo!!

Ah . . . . ah . . . . ah . . . . ah . . . . Stayin' Alive . . . . Stayin' Alive . . . . Ah . . . . ah . . . . ah . . . . ah . . . . Stayin' Aliiiiiii . . . iiiiiii . . . . iiiiiii . . . . iiiiiiive . . . .
Do . . . . do . . . . do . . . . do . . . . do . . . . do . . . . do.do.do . . . . do . . . . do . . . . do . . . . do . . . . do . . . . do.do!

I apologize in advance for the suffering you will endure not being able to get that song out of your head for the next few days!

Hey, I'm on the other side of this thing! In the middle of chemo, I thought this day would never come! Again, I held onto you all and your prayers!! Thank you, dear Lord, for these precious friends!! I owe my very life to them!! Please, bless each and every one of them!!

Well, it's getting late and I'm beat, but I had to let you in on my celebration, and by golly, I hope to celebrate with each of you soon!!

With More Love and Thanks One Person Can Muster,
Carrie

Here's a better song to put into your head:

Thou hast turned for me my mourning into dancing:
Thou hast put off my sackcloth, and girded me with gladness;
To the end that my glory may sing praise to thee, and not be silent.
O Lord my God, I will give thanks unto thee for ever.

Psalm 30:11-12

ALOHA!

8/18/08

Man, oh man! I forgot how busy life can get when you're healthy. Granted, I'm making up for lost time! J.T., Max and I just had a very fun week! I put off writing you all, because I wanted to spend as much time with the boys as possible. Paul is taking them on a two week vacation starting today. Yes, that would be my family going on vacation . . . without me. A friend said having a spouse leave you, and the whole separation/divorce thing is like walking around with an open wound. Very profound! That is exactly what it feels like. I'm attempting to make lemonade out of lemons by taking a vacation of my own to Hawaii with a dear friend. You'll be able to find us on the beaches of Oahu drinking . . . what else? . . . the lemonade!

I saw my doctor last week, and we went over my scans. My PET scan shows no cancer!! Wohoo! My CT scan shows the same enlarged lymph nodes as before. I must admit—the doc used the word "radiation" a few times more than I would have liked. If those swollen nodes get any larger, it's Radiation Diaries time. My next scans will be in January. There is a good chance those lymph nodes will stay the same size forever. If the Lord has taught me nothing else, it's take a day at a time and don't take my eyes off Him!

Just pray for the doctor who ever mentions the word "chemotherapy" to me again—they're a goner!

Well, this trip is my last hurrah before taking my plethora of pills. Stay tuned for the <u>Szulgai Diaries</u> coming your way after Labor Day. Thank you so much for your prayers for the cancer, the lymph nodes, the m. szulgai, and of course, the open wound. I love you all, and you are always in my prayers!!

Love & Blessings,
Carrie

Before the mountains were born or You had brought forth the earth and the world, from everlasting to everlasting You are God.

Psalm 90:2

THE SZULGAI DIARIES:
THE BEGINNING

9/8/08

Hi Everyone!!

I am hoping this finds you well!! I wanted to let you know that I had a wonderful trip to Hawaii!! Very relaxing! Just what I needed! My energy is coming back bit by bit. After what I went through, I feel like a super hero—call me Egghead Woman! Actually, my hair is coming back bit by bit, also. If you are ever feeling down, just shave your head. People are so nice to you!! I'm actually going to miss that extra bit of attention (and, I'm sure, prayers)! I'll be sure to keep that Gillette shaver on hand—just in case I need a pick-me-up!

Regarding the ol' m. szulgai, one of the pills made me very sick (memories of the chemo nausea came rushing back), so we are going to try something else this week. I see Dr. Infectious Disease tomorrow, so I'll keep you posted!

Thank you for your prayers, and know that you are in mine!!

Much, much love,
Carrie

Blessed be the Lord, who daily loads us with benefits, even the God of our salvation.

Psalm 68:19

THE SZULGAI DIARIES: THE END?

9/10/08

Yessss! My infectious disease doctor thinks we should wait to see if I ever get any symptoms of this disease before I take any more pills. I thoroughly agree! These pills are so toxic they can cause damage to your eyes, your liver, not to mention the plethora of side effects. So I am soooo happy! As I said before, this disease may sit there and never affect me—ever. Soooo if I come to mind any time in the future, please throw up a prayer for the disappearance of the mycobacterium szulgai. You can call it "the bug", and I'm sure the Lord will know what you're talking about. Just say no to "the bug"!

I also saw my oncologist. I told him I felt great and full of energy! He said, "Really, because you're still anemic and some blood counts are still low." You know what this means don't you—MORE energy is coming!! Wohoo! It's a volleyball, it's a balloon, NO . . . IT'S EGGHEAD WOMAN!! Able to eggs-plore beyond the boundaries of her home and Mission Hospital! Able to scramble the minds of many! Able to crack up at all bad jokes, uh make that yolks! Okay, enough of the egg humor! I have actually accomplished hat hair and bed head this past week! Thank you, thank you!! It's the little things that you love after cancer—and that is very true!!

Love you much,
Carrie

It is a good thing to give thanks unto the Lord,
and to sing praises unto thy name, O most High;
To show forth thy lovingkindness in the morning,
and thy faithfulness every night.

Psalm 92:1-2

AN IDENTITY CRISIS

10/7/08

Hi Everyone!!

I have a story for you: Last week I was grocery shopping and a sweet lady stopped me. "Chemo patient, eh?" She recognized the hairdo. We talked for a while. She is a breast cancer survivor of 14 years (that's a beautiful thing). Before we parted she said, "Well, you look great! You look like a model!" So I spent the rest of the day pretending I looked like Heidi Klum.

The next day I was sitting in my car with my boys at a drive thru. I was turned sideways talking to Max, when the attendant said, "Excuse me, Sir!" I turned around, and she sheepishly replied, "Uh, sorry." I went from super model to male impersonator within 24 hours. Auf wiedersehen, Heidi!

I saw my oncologist today, and things are fine. I'm still anemic and all my blood counts have gone down a bit, so pray for my blood and my lungs. Otherwise, I am feeling better and better everyday! I'm off to eat a big steak dinner (doctor's orders, and all)!

Much Love & Blessings,
Carrie

But seek ye first the kingdom of God, and his righteousness; and all these things shall be added unto you.

Matthew 6:25-33

WHAT I'M THANKFUL FOR

11/26/08

That title has to go, because there are not enough megabytes in our computers to hold all the things I am thankful for this year!

It is unbelievable how chemotherapy seems like a distant memory. When I visit my doctor and walk by the chemo room, it feels like I could have never really been in there. It's hard not to cry for those dear people. It brings me to my knees in prayer for them (and yes, for me and everyone I know) every time!!

I will say that the new appreciation of life is unbelievable, also!! It's not so much an appreciation of life as an appreciation of each day. "New every morning" is the best way I can describe it!

A VERY FEW things I am thankful for:

God's gift of -

YOU

My family

Wonderful doctors

Wonderful medical employees in general

Let's not forget medical insurance

Each day without cancer

More importantly, each day without chemotherapy

Okay, chemotherapy—it was the cure after all

Breathing without coughing—Yessssss!

My dog—my fellow napper for 6 months

Life without and with hair—both have their advantages

Comfort food—milkshakes, submarine sandwiches, hamburgers—this could be the reason Carrie did not lose weight while on chemo.

HGTV—I can now redecorate anyone's home in one week or less

DVDs—how were we ever sick without them? The goldfish idea would have buried me for sure!

Knowing God is in control in the midst of "the wilderness"!

Again, it's countless!! Let me just say, yet again, I would NOT have made it through this year without you!! Have a most incredible Thanksgiving!!

Love and Blessings,
Carrie

O Give thanks unto the Lord; for he is good: for his mercy endures forever!

Psalm 136:1

SINGLE WOMEN—REJOICE!

12/8/08

Hi Everyone!

Well, the hair is growing, but I haven't quite reached the hair length of an average person. The evidence is how extremely nice the general public is to me along with the fact that all my friend's children are praying that my hair grows.

I have a story (if you are a single female—this is for you). My television recently died, so I went to Costco to get a new one. Girls, if you want to capture the attention of every male around you, simply walk around with a flat screen TV in your shopping cart. It was comical! Six months ago I was half dead from chemo and bald—would anyone help me get my groceries in my car? Last week I heard, "Let me help you get that TV in your car, miss!" from across the parking lot. My new discovery—forget beauty and brains—simply strap a flat screen TV box on your back!!

Silly, I know!! I had an encouraging Lung Doctor appointment! I had another Pulmonary Function Test and everything looked better! That's what happens when you have great prayer partners!! Thanks you, dear friends, and thank you, Lord!!

I hope you are all enjoying the craziness of the season, and celebrating the miracle of Christ's birth!

Much Love & Blessings,
Carrie

Charm is deceitful and beauty is vain, but a woman who fears the Lord, she shall be praised.

Proverbs 31:30

(thought I'd better include that verse with this one)

MERRY CHRISTMAS!

12/22/08

Ahhhh! Christmas emails! What a beautiful invention!! I would like to share with you my favorite of the season which has absolutely no deep meaning whatsoever. But it's funny!

The wife has been on my case to get the Christmas lights up for a couple of weeks. They are up now and for some reason she will not talk to me . . .

I'm doing this next year!! You can call it "my own personal stand against Christmas commercialism" (or "Scrooge") whichever you prefer.

Just wanted to let you know how thankful I am for you all this Christmas!! I am feeling especially blessed this year!!

You are in my heart, and thoughts and prayers!! God bless you and your families!

Much, Much Love,
Carrie

Today in the town of David a Savior has been born to you; he is Christ the Lord.

Luke 2:11

(Deep meaning in this—Amen?)

HAPPY, HAPPY NEW YEAR!

1/26/09

Hi Everyone!!

I hope you all had a wonderful Christmas! A good friend told me how happy she was that she was a Christian, because she could celebrate Christ's birth all year round! Amen to that sister, because it ain't gonna happen during the Christmas season—that's for sure!! My goodness—I find my head spinning with the gifts, decorations, trees, and let's not forget, the Christmas goodies!! Oh my!! I love that she said that, and by golly, I'm going to break out into "Joy to the World" right now!!

I had an appointment with my oncologist last week, and my blood counts are going up! Yessss! I rode with this darling older couple on the elevator. She burst out with, "I've been cancer free for five years!', and he followed that with, "We're going out for steak and a milkshake!" Ahhh, people after my own heart! I considered stowing away in the trunk of their car.

I have a big prayer request for you—next week, February 3—I revisit my "favorite place" for my scans. Again, pray that I can lie perfectly still for one hour without breaking into "The Mexican Hat Dance" half way through. Specifically, pray that there is no cancer, and that my swollen lymph nodes are the same size (or smaller). I'll let you know the results as soon as I get them!!

I hope this email finds you all well, and enjoying the new year. It is going to be interesting to go through the events of this year, and remembering where I was last year. Makes each day that much more wonderful—beautiful—words can't describe it!!

Much Love and Blessings,
Carrie

O Lord, open thou my lips;
and my mouth shall shew forth thy praise.

Psalm 51:15

CANCER—PART II

SOS: SAVE OUR SISTER!

2/9/09

Hi Everyone!

Time to put on that prayer warrior *sword and shield*. No boring prayer lives for **my** prayer partners!!

Here is the scoop—Everything we were working on curing last year is cured, **however**, the PET scan showed something **new** (in my chest). Oh boy! We're not sure if it's cancer or an infection (may be the mycobacterium szulgai). They won't know until they do surgery, and go in there and get a sample. Once we know what it is, we can move forward with the treatment.

Well, there you have it. Not the report I was hoping to give, but it is what it is. I've just got to stick with my motto—Day at a time & eyes on God!! I meet with my oncologist tomorrow, and will fill you in on any details I get. I'll also be meeting with the surgeon soon.

I'll probably write you tomorrow. My big request right now is that "peace that surpasses understanding". Thank you all!

God bless you!
Carrie

Bend down, O Lord, and hear my prayer; answer me, for I need your help.

Psalm 86:1

WHAT TO PRAY FOR

2/10/09

Hi Everyone!

I saw my oncologist today, and I now know EXACTLY what it is I need prayer for. I meet with the surgeon tomorrow morning, and hopefully, he will do the biopsy (in my lungs) SOON! If it turns out to be my infectious disease—the myco-blah-ba-de-blah-blah—I go back to taking my truckload of toxic pills. If it's more lymphoma—EEK—I get to move to the City of Hope where I'll be getting **new, more aggressive** doses of chemotherapy and a bone marrow transplant. Soooo, we all know exactly what to pray for, eh? Toxic pills are looking like a beautiful thing!!

My other motto in life—don't cross that bridge until you get there—is coming in pretty handy right now. I AM feeling that peace!! I can't thank you enough for your prayers!! I got so many wonderful emails yesterday—I was able to go to sleep last night thinking, "I am loved and not alone in this". Seriously, I went to sleep in perfect peace! Miracle workers you are!!

I'll let you know tomorrow when my surgery will be. God bless you, precious partners!!!

Sure Love You!!
Carrie

I praise You because I am fearfully
and wonderfully made;
Your works are wonderful,
I know that full well.

Psalm 139:14

DOOR NUMBER THREE

2/11/09

Hi Everyone!

I met with the surgeon today. Totally nice guy! The Lord has surrounded me with the nicest doctors. I feel very well taken care of!! My surgery is next Wednesday at 11:30 a.m. They are going in my side and taking out a lymph node under my lung. I will be in the hospital for the next day or two (Saddleback Memorial), and the results will come in 3-7 days after the surgery. Some good news—he said there is a chance it is just a benign blob (an old infection or something like that).

So behind Door #1 we have—Big time suffering

Behind Door #2 we have—Small time suffering

And behind Door #3 we have—No suffering

I'll be the first to admit that there are some beautiful lessons to be learned with suffering, **however**, let's pray Carrie has learned all her "suffering lessons". Oh Lord, I'm ready for Door #3 . . . right? He's in control of my life and that's a wonderful thing!! I can't thank you all enough for your supportive emails! Right now we have everything covered (God bless my parents). If things go the way of Door #1,

I will surely be hitting you up for any help you offer!! So thank you, again!!!!!

Well, it's wonderful knowing I have hundreds of people praying for a benign lymph node BLOB!! The peace surrounding me is THICK—I FEEL it!!!

Words cannot express my gratitude and my love for you all!! God Bless You, Guys!!

Much Love,
Carrie

Peace I leave with you, my peace I give unto you: not as the world gives, give I unto you. Let not your heart be troubled, neither let it be afraid.

John 14:27

GIVE ME A "B"

2/17/09

Okay, Everyone!! Get your prayer warrior pom-poms and repeat after me:

Give me a "B"!

Give me a "9"!

What's that spell?..Benign!!!

What's that spell?..Benign!!!

Rah! Rah! Rah!

This is our prayer (not the results—yet) for the next week or so!!

Tomorrow is my surgery at 11:30 am, and I'm feeling the PEACE!! I always look forward to anesthesia! 24 hours of sleep-count me in!!

I thank you all so much for your prayers!! You're the best!! You know I'll write you the SECOND I get the results!!

I love you much!!

Love & Blessings,
Carrie

You will keep in perfect peace
him whose mind is steadfast,
because he trusts in you.

Isaiah 26:3

THE HOSPITAL OF HORRORS

2/19/09

Hi Everyone!!

Well, believe it or not, I'm home already!! The surgical procedure went well, and I'm recovering nicely, HOWEVER, I have found the ultimate torture device for any POW Camp. It's called the **chest tube**. If you've had one, you know what I'm talking about—the crying, the screaming, "More Morphine!! More Morphine!!" My nurses even called my doctor at midnight and asked, "More Morphine? More Morphine?" Thankfully, my doctor responded, "YES!! More Morphine!! More Morphine!!" I would like to personally meet the inventor of this drug and thank him!! The morphine (barely) got me through the night, and when my doctor took out that tube (excuse me, garden hose) this morning, I was a new person—the sun was shining, the birds were singing, and I was shouting Hallelujah!!

Whew!! I am feeling MUCH better, and the doc said they may have the results of that lymph node he took out by tomorrow—so stay tuned.

Well, what's there to fear? I feel so completely prayed over by you all, and God's in control! God BLESS you guys!!

I dearly love you,
Carrie

Fear not, for I have redeemed you; I have summoned you by name; you are mine.

When you pass through the waters, I will be with you; when you pass through the rivers,

they will not sweep over you. When you walk through the fire, you will not be burned;

the flames will not set you ablaze. For I am the Lord, your God, the Holy One of Israel, your Savior.

Isaiah 43:1-3

DOOR NUMBER ONE—OH MY!

2/25/09

I was hoping for the NEW CAR behind door number 3, but instead got the donkey and the cart behind door number 1. But seriously, if ol' Beelzebub thinks he is doing himself a favor by giving me more cancer, he's more pathetic than I thought!! Instead of hundreds, we will probably have thousands lifting our voices in prayer!! Instead of hundreds of reasons, I will probably have thousands more reasons to ask for prayer (oh my), but with that I hope to help lift people's eyes towards God through His wonderful Word. And think of all the opportunity there is to serve out there—OHHHHH—I thank you in advance.

A beautiful story—yesterday I was a bundle of nerves waiting for a phone call from my doctor, which never came. This morning I had an appt. with him, and as I was getting ready to go, I heard the audible voice of God (this has only happened twice before, and He seems to **know** when we need to hear it). "Carrie, I need a correspondent at the City of Hope." After a HUGE SIGH from me I said, "Okay Lord, I'm your gal." So I knew what I was going to hear this morning, and with that was the extraordinary comfort that I am in the center of God's will. So I don't doubt I will be coming to you LIVE FROM THE CITY OF HOPE—I'm a girl on a mission!!

I have left messages with my oncologist's office. I'll need them to tell me what my next step is. When my doctor said I'll be moving to the City of Hope, I don't know if he meant for one week or six months. So as soon as I find out the scoop I will let you know.

My immediate prayer requests:

1) That lymphoma will learn to HATE my body!!
2) Oi!! The logistics of "moving out"—my boys, my dog, the ten million loose ends to tie!! Gets my head spinning!!
3) Quick healing from last week's surgery—so I can have a bit of fun before I hit the Chamber of Torture, ah excuse me, I meant City of Hope!

Wow!! This disease didn't give me much of a break, but there is a reason for everything. Let's keep looking up, and when I can't lift my head any longer, you can hold my chin up for me!!! Thank you, thank you my dear friends!

Love & Blessings,
Carrie

Casting all your care upon Him;
for He careth for you.

I Peter 5:7

SIDE-SPLITTING HUMOR

2/26/09

Last night some of my closest friends took me out to dessert to cheer me up. (Earlier that day my doctor took out the stitches from my side.) My friends and I were having a great time at the restaurant talking and laughing. I was laughing so hard that all of a sudden I felt a waterfall of *something* running down my side. Sure enough, it was blood. I felt so sorry for the restaurant customers that night.

One of my friends sped me off to the ER where we waited for hours for a doctor to spend 2 minutes super-gluing my side back together. We **did** have entertainment, however. The ER was so crowded that many patients, including myself, had to hang out in the hallway instead of a room. My friend and I had a hard time NOT watching a man throw up literally hundreds of times just 20 feet away from us. Do I know how to show my friends a good time or what?

Here's to having "knee slapping" instead of "side splitting" jokes!!

Much Love,
Carrie

Do not rejoice over me, my enemy!
Though I have fallen, I will stand up.
Though I sit in darkness,
The Lord will be my light.

Micah 7:8

PATIENCE IS A VIRTUE

3/4/09

Granted, it's not a virtue **I** possess!! Just kidding, I'm learning!! Anyway, I finally heard from the City of Hope and have an appointment with the Big Cheese Lymphoma Doctor on Friday. I am so curious to hear where this "adventure" is going to take me. I looked up "Bone Marrow Transplant" on the internet (I recall advising you all not to do this kind of thing—do as I say, not as I do), and that was enlightening! I thought as a strong Christian I was going to be able to avoid hell, but according to the internet that may not be the case. I bet there's a lot of chocolate at the City of Hope.

I am secretly hoping the Lord's words to me ("I need a correspondent at the City of Hope") are an "Abraham, I want you to sacrifice your son" kind of thing. I'm looking for a sacrificial ram everywhere I go (if you don't know what on Earth I'm talking about, read Genesis 22:1-18). So, if any of you know of a ram that needs a bone marrow transplant, be sure to let me know.

Enough silliness, I'm doing well!! I still have quite the pain in my chest from my biopsy. Last week I asked the doctor why I was still in such pain, and he said, "Oh, you could have pain for EIGHT weeks." Okay, THAT explains that!! So that leads me to my current prayer requests:

1) Of course, faster healing than 8 weeks (I'm on week two) from my surgery.

2) Praise God, he has already prepared me for pretty much everything I'm going to hear on Friday. Pray that any surprises are good news (like—what's that ram doing stuck in those bushes outside?).

3) That the Lord would continue to go ahead of me and prepare the STUFF I need to coordinate in the future (Again, Praise Him—He is already on the move working in people, places and things!!)

4) J.T. and Max. Again, thank you, Lord! They are doing so well! Pray they hold onto God during their Mom's roller coaster ride.

Again, I have NOT felt alone in this!! You are all such a blessing!! I will probably update you on Friday, and let you know the scoop. I love you all, and am praying for you!

Much, Much Love,
Carrie

Who shall separate us from the love of Christ? Shall tribulation, or distress, or persecution, or famine, or nakedness, or peril, or sword?

Romans 8:35

WHO HAS INCREDIBLE
PRAYER PARTNERS?

3/6/09

That would be me!! Just got back from the City of Hope with some wonderful news!! I will be getting a Stem Cell Transplant and not a Bone Marrow Transplant!! Wohoo! This means way less suffering involved! Here is my time line, and bear with me, I may not have heard EVERYTHING correctly:

3/10/09-3/13/09 I'm at City of Hope getting killer chemotherapy. Nausea, hair loss, the whole bit. I'll be the one yelling, "More drugs! More drugs!!"

3/31/09-4/3/09 A repeat of above. I'll also be getting a bone marrow biopsy, lung tests, heart tests, and I will have surgery for a "Hickman" catheter.

4/13/09—approximately 4/17/09 I'm at City of Hope where they will be harvesting my stem cells. This is where the "Hickman" comes in. The doctor said it works similar to dialysis. They gave me a book to read—I'll educate you as I learn, because I KNOW you are all over learning about stem cell transplants!!

One week later—I'm at the City of Hope for about one month. During this time, I will be getting more killer chemo, the stem cell transplant, and then recover.

The doctor said if all goes well, I should be done by mid-May. "MID-MAY!!" I almost jumped out of my chair with joy!! I thought for sure this was going to be another LONG, DRAWN-OUT experience like last year. Bring on the short term suffering!! YESSSSSS!

They also advised me to bring a laptop computer if I have one!! This means I get to bring all of you to the hospital with me!! THAT is a beautiful thing!! My next correspondence will be LIVE FROM THE CITY OF HOPE! Wait, where have I heard that before? Is God good, or what?

What can I say? I have the best prayer partners!! Let's sing Hallelujah together!! I love you, guys, and I'll be talking to you soon!!

Much Love,
Carrie

I will praise thee, O Lord, with my whole heart;
I will shew forth all thy marvelous works.
I will be glad and rejoice in thee:
I will sing praise to thy name, O thou most High.
Psalm 9: 1-2

MEMORIES . . .
MAY BE BEAUTIFUL AND . . . YET

3/13/09

What's too painful to remember—Sing it Barbra!!
We simply choose to forget—Oh I want to forget!!

I'm okay! I survived! This round of chemo included minimal nausea and about 30 hours of sleeping—yeah, that would be almost straight through. So needless to say, I'm going to owe my prayer partners BIG TIME!! You're the best!! Alas, I could not figure out how to get on the internet at City of Hope being the techo-savvy person I am. Hopefully, I'll get it right by May.

I have to run up to COH tomorrow for an injection. I asked if I could do it myself at home like I did last year. "No dear, this shot costs $5,000.00". Alrighty, then! I will also be going back to the COH on 3/24 for my bone marrow biopsy. Then back again 3/31 for my next chemo round. Thank you so much for praying for each of these events! Please also pray for my parents and others who will be driving me back and forth (one hour plus each way with no traffic—God bless them!!)

I have a new POW Camp torture for the hard of hearing (not that I am hard of hearing, mind you!) Imagine four days where the only people who talk to you are wearing face masks—muffling every word they say and hiding all facial expressions and lip movements). Maybe that's why I slept so much—the mental exhaustion!

Keep praying for the pain in my chest from the surgery—feels a bit worse. Thank you so much!!

Much Love & Blessings,
Carrie

Blessed is the man that trusteth in the Lord,
and whose hope the Lord is.

Jeremiah 17:7

AND THEY CALL HER—
EL BARFO!!!

3/17/09

Okay, when I was in the hospital, there must be something to having those meds. pumped straight into the IV tube. Since I've been home, if I don't have the right combo of meds. and food in my stomach—Thar she blows!! I think things are getting better since I've had my first incident free day (granted, it's not over yet). Nausea LOVES me—alas!

A story—My 15 year old (J.T.) has not been a "cuddler" for quite a long time, and he chose to drive with my parents and I up to the COH last Saturday when I got my shot. It was a "Master Card" moment:

Fuel for the drive to Duarte—$6.00
Cost of shot in the arm—$5,000.00
Cuddling with your 15 year old for 2 hours—priceless!

Last year Max stayed overnight in the hospital to help take care of me! Sometimes being missed by your kids is a great thing! I sure have memories that will last a lifetime!

A friend of mine shared this with me—it is delightful—I just wanted to pass it along to you:

The Road of Life

At first, I saw God as my observer,
my judge,
keeping track of the things I did wrong,
so as to know whether I merited heaven
or hell when I die.
He was out there sort of like a president.
I recognized His picture when I saw it,
but I really didn't know Him.
But later on when I met Christ,
It seemed as though life were rather like a bike ride,
But it was a tandem bike,
And I noticed that Christ
was in the back helping me pedal.
I don't know just when it was
that He suggested we change places,
But life has not been the same since.
When I had control,
I knew the way.
It was rather boring,
But predictable . . .
It was the shortest distance between two points.
But when He took the lead,
He knew delightful long cuts,
Up mountains,
And through rocky places
At breakneck speeds,
It was all I could do to hang on!
Even though it looked like madness,
He said, "Pedal!"
I worried and was anxious
And asked,

"Where are you taking me?"
He laughed and didn't answer,
And I started to learn to trust.
         I forgot my boring life
And entered into the adventure.
And when I'd say, "I'm scared,"
He'd lean back and touch my hand.
         He took me to people with gifts that I needed,
Gifts of healing, acceptance
And joy.
They gave me gifts to take on my journey,
My Lord's and mine.
         And we were off again.
He said, "Give the gifts away;
They're extra baggage, too much weight."
So I did,
To the people we met,
And I found that in giving I received,
And still our burden was light.
         I did not trust Him,
At first,
In control of my life.
I thought He'd wreck it;
But He knows the bike secrets,
Knows how to make it bend to take sharp corners,
Knows how to jump to clear high rocks,
Knows how to fly to shorten scary passages.
         And I am learning to shut up
And pedal
In the strangest places,
And I'm beginning to enjoy the view
And the cool breeze on my face

With my delightful constant companion, Jesus Christ.
And when I'm sure I just can't do anymore,
He just smiles and says . . . "Pedal."

—Author unknown

I **love** that!!

Thank you for your prayers!! Next Tuesday I have my bone marrow biopsy—I will be sedated, so I won't feel a thing. I'll keep you posted!

Love & Blessings,
Carrie

He maketh me to lie down in green pastures;
He leadeth me beside the still waters.

Psalm 23:2

KEEP PEDALING, CARRIE!

3/25/09

Remember that cute poem I sent you last week? Welllllll, The Lord is on the front of that tandem bicycle yelling, "Faster!", and Carrie has found herself in the back yelling, "BRAKES!"

First, I want to let you know that my Bone Marrow Biopsy went smoothly. I only have a little soreness in my back. Also, the soreness in my side from February's surgery is feeling better. It is healing oh-so-gradually, but at least it's getting better.

After my bone marrow biopsy, I spoke with a nurse about my surgery next week when they install my Hickman Catheter. When she showed me this thing, I thought you've GOT to be kidding me. It looks like something out of "Plan Nine from Outer Space!" The catheter runs into your heart, and she informed me that during the surgery a small percentage of patients accidentally have the catheter hit the lung. At this point you have a few more days in the hospital with a **chest tube**. "BRAKES!" I told her if this happens, I want the surgical team to pull all the plugs and just let me go!! I don't think she understood the sincerity of my request!

Then I took a class on how to take care of my new science fiction apparatus. The teacher started the session by asking, "Do any of you have a friend or relative who is a registered nurse?" You get the picture—she then proceeded to give us a crash course in nursing in which I felt only a LITTLE more confident than the guy sitting next to me who could not speak a word of English. Lord, please don't let me pump an air bubble into my heart!!

I know the Lord is calling from the front seat saying, "Fear not, Carrie!" Okay, but I think He knows I'm going to be riding the next couple of months with my eyes closed!

I am speechless again in how thankful I am for you!! You are helping me pedal, when I cannot!!

Love and Blessings,
Carrie

God is not a man, that He should lie;
neither the son of man, that He should repent;
hath He said, and shall He not do it?
or hath He spoken,
and shall He not make it good?

Numbers 23:19

HAIR TODAY—GONE TOMORROW

3/30/09

"Are not five sparrows sold for two pennies? Yet not one of them is forgotten by God.
Indeed, the very hairs of your head are all numbered.
Don't be afraid; you are worth more than many sparrows"

Luke 12:6-7

Well, Carrie is feeling quite special to God this week. I **love** you all, but frankly, I could care less how many hairs you have on you head! God was counting with me as I lost them—5,034-5,035—etc. His attention to detail, and love for us is overwhelming!! This verse definitely helped my second experience of losing all my hair, which as you can imagine, is just gross!

Last year I had some fighter hairs that didn't give up the battle to stay in my scalp. This year they are losing the fight! It won't be long until the top of my head resembles a planet! Right now my head (with it's few long hairs left) looks like something you'd find in a Halloween yard sale!

Well, I'm off to City of Hope tomorrow for the rest of the week. It's going to be a hopping time—CT scan, chemo, surgery! Yeah! Keep pedaling for me, Lord!! My biggest prayer request is that I don't need a chest tube after the surgery! One experience of that in my lifetime was quite enough!! And, of course, there is always the request that the chemo is working—we'll find that out through the CT scan.

Thank you for your prayers for J.T. and Max. They are doing great! I will be in and out of the hospital in April and stay there almost the whole month of May. I am going to miss them and sure appreciate your prayers for them during this time!! Also, thank you for your prayers for my caregivers—my parents and friends—they are carrying me right along—helping me pedal!!

I will keep you posted! I will probably keep my laptop at home this round (if memory serves, I will be sleeping the next four days, which suits me fine), so I will probably write next week-end!!

"Treasure the one who lightens
the burden of anyone else."

Charles Dickens

I **treasure** you all!! God bless you, guys!!

Much, Much Love,
Carrie

PEDALING THROUGH THE SEA

4/6/09

As I found the Lord and I (on our tandem bicycle) coming up to the Sea of Despair, I yelled, "Hey, I bet there is sturdy ground if we go AROUND this thing." Splash!! Right into the water we go! I'm sure He knows what He's doing—no doubt it is the ONLY way to the other side!! "Keep pedaling!" I hear Him say. "Yeah, Lord, I'd hate to miss the Nausea Swim Up Pool Bar, the Piranha Shots I have to give myself and that pitiful feeling I get when dealing with my Hickman—I'm looking for a Registered Nurse Shark!" He laughs at my attempt at sarcasm! I trust Him, so through the Sea it is!!

There it is—those are all the highlights of my day! Oh boy!! I have never actually "Xed" out days of the calendar, but I'm doing it now!!

Please let me pause to let you know how thankful I am for your prayers. EVERYTHING is going as it is supposed to:

My bone marrow is clean!

The chemo is shrinking my tumors!

I DIDN'T have to have a chest tube inserted in to my body! Hallelujah!!

My Hickman catheter is looking good, as far as there being no infection! Actually, it LOOKS like I should be picking up radio waves from outer space.

And mentally I know the Sea is temporary.

I thank you so much!!! I just wanted to give you an update, and I'll write more when I'm out of the Sea—about 3-4 days. In the meantime, thank you a million for pedaling for me!!

Much Love and Blessings,
Carrie

My flesh and my heart faileth:
but God is the strength of my heart,
and my portion forever.

Psalm 73:26

CHEMO—SCHMEMO!

4/10/09

I want to inform you that last Thanksgiving I must have had a **major** brain cramp when I said I was thankful for chemotherapy. We have GOT to start praying for a better cure!! Oh, my!! I'm feeling better today! Thank you, Lord!!

Some Prayer Requests:

Monday I go to the COH, and they will be harvesting my stem cells. This usually takes 3-10 days. My request is, of course, that it takes 1-2 days!! They then freeze them, and I hope to find out why this makes them as good as new as opposed to boiling them or letting them dry out in the sun.

I'm home for a week, and then it's back to the COH for about 3 1/2 weeks. This will be the dark before the dawn—killer chemo, the transplant, and then recovery! Oh Lord, please let this work—for a very, very long time!!

I KNOW God is in control, I just WANT Him to be in control without the involvement of chemo!!

I love you, guys!! Thank you so much for everything you've done for me!!

"It's not what we have in our life, but who we have in our life that counts."

J.M. Laurence

I am blessed!!!!

Love & Blessings,
Carrie

This third I will bring into the fire;
I will refine them like silver and test them like gold.
They will call on my name and I will answer them;
I will say, "They are my people,"
And they will say, "The Lord is our God."

Zechariah 13:9

Since I am being refined by chemotherapy, I have a fear of ending up like Pizza the Hut.

LIVE FROM THE CITY OF HOPE

4/13/09

Hi Everyone!!

I'm finally coming to you from the COH—so happy I've figured this out!! Thank you so very, very much for your prayers.

Here is yet another "all about me" request—Oh man, did I have a horrible first day at the stem cell harvesting machine today!! Let me just say the nurses there have named me the "incredible barfing woman". Nausea is a possible side effect, and as we know, nausea LOVES me!! Ahhhhh! It's a five hour ordeal, and I thought boredom was going to be my big concern. Bring on the boredom!!! Please pray this ends soon!! Thank you, thank you!!

Much Love & Blessings,
Carrie

O Lord, hear my prayer;
Listen to my supplications;
In Thy faithfulness and
In Thy righteousness answer me.

Psalm 143:1

I OWE YOU ONE!

4/14/09

Rarely does anyone give over 5 million stem cells in **two** days, but those people do NOT have my prayer partners!!! I found out that yesterday I gave 3.3 million stem cells, and the chances of topping the 5 million mark today are extremely good!! I find out around 11:00 am tomorrow. I'll be calling the lab with my bags packed and one foot out the door.

Thank you, Lord!! And thank you all so much for your prayers!!! I was nauseous today, but at least I was not Barfina!! I had to get a blood transfusion and a platelet transfusion after the stem cell harvesting, so that was 9 hours of me lying in a bed with tubes in me—ga, ga, ga—I'm going a little crazy. Makes me that much happier that I'm probably going home tomorrow!!!

Well, it's late. I just wanted you to rejoice with me!! Thank you so much!! I love you, guys!!

Much Love,
Carrie

Rejoice in the Lord always:
And again I say, Rejoice.

Philippians 4:4

KEEP PEDALING EVERYONE!

4/22/09

Hi Everyone!!

Well, I didn't want to let another day go by without a long list of prayer requests for ya!!

But FIRST a "Glory Hallelujah!" for the 6.1 million stem cells in two days!! Wohoo! Even the nurses in the donor room were happy to see me (barf bag lady) go!! I'll tell you—those two days made me mental—God was MERCIFUL!!!

They told me I would be weak/tired from the event, and I'm learning a whole new meaning of the word "rest" which wasn't in my vocabulary before January of 2008!! I feel fairly energetic today, and so, I am up and writing!!

*Okay, first request—Friday at 6:45 a.m. I have a pet scan at the COH. Please pray that the results are what the doctor is looking for (smaller/no tumors).

*Next, I will be checking into the COH for my 3 1/2 week "vacation" on Tuesday 4/28. I'm not sure exactly when these will occur, but I'll be getting the chemo to kill everything—bad and good cells alike—the stem cell transplant, and recovery. So if you just pray for the entire stay . . .

*Pray for little pain, little nausea, and nurses who give lots of drugs!! Bottom line—please pray that this works!! The whole process is amazing!!

*Lastly, please pray for J.T. and Max.

Please know that I am praying for all of you, too. My goodness, I think almost everyone on my list is facing something. Let's all keep pedaling! If you have to, do like me and close your eyes knowing God is in control!!

I'm hoping to have my laptop up and running when I get to COH! O BOY, minute by minute prayer requests!! Seriously, I look forward to hearing from you! I love you guys so much!!

Much Love,
Carrie

I will bless the Lord at all times: His praise shall continually be in my mouth. My soul shall make her boast in the Lord; let the humble hear it and be glad. Magnify the Lord with me and let us exalt His name together. I sought the Lord and He answered me and freed me from all my fears.

Psalm 34: 1-4

MY SCHEDULE OF FUN

4/29/09

Hi Everyone!!

Now I am praying for what wonderful thing I can do for **you**!! The cancer is gone!! Yessssssss! This is exactly what the doctors needed to move ahead with the stem cell transplant. Wohoo!! So now we just need to kill off any last bad cells and put in my shiny, new stem cells.

Yesterday, I moved into my beautiful room on the sixth floor. I have a view of the quarry and the 605 FWY. The staff here is BEYOND nice!!

Here is my schedule:

4/29-5/1 Carmustine Chemo

5/2 Etoposide Chemo

5/4 Cyclophosphamide Chemo

(for those of you who are chemo savvy)

5/6 Stem Cell Transplant

I'll give you more facts on the recovery process later. Looks like a fun time, eh? I guess the Cyclop-blah-ba-de-blah-blah is an especially nasty chemo. You in the anti-nausea ministry have your work cut out for you!

I'll be in touch probably more than you would like me to!!

Love & Blessings,
Carrie

For indeed He was crucified by reason of weakness, but lives because of God's power. For we also are weak in him, but we will live together with Him, because of God's power toward you.

2 Corinthians 13:4

THE BEAUTY OF A
DRUG INDUCED COMA

5/2/09

Hi Everyone!!

I have received so many inspiring and encouraging emails from you guys, I just have to write all of you and say thank you SO MUCH!! Your prayers are being answered!

I LIKE this place! Besides having some of the most wonderful people working here, they have done a beautiful job of keeping me sleeping 20 hours a day. It's a good way to stay sane!!

I have had three of my chemos so far and have two to go. I guess the next two are nausealicious, so keep those prayers coming!!

In my stupor, I'm praying for you all!! I love you, and I'll be in touch!! God bless you and your families!!

All My Love,
Carrie

He will be very gracious unto thee at the voice of thy cry, when He shall hear it, He will answer thee.

Isaiah 30:19

DOWN IN THE VALLEY

5/5/09

After 5 days of dreadful chemo (the last two were a complete nightmare), I was sitting here feeling nauseous, blue, exhausted, a mere fraction of the person I was a few days ago. Then I read YOUR emails. Every word from every one of you encouraged and inspired me!! I was feeling pretty defeated, but not any more!! God is good!!

Tomorrow is my Stem Cell Transplant, so right now all my blood counts are about as low as can be. So there's only one way to go and that's up—starting tomorrow! I'll write more when I'm feeling better!!

Thank you earnestly for your prayers!! They are getting me through this!!

Love you with all my heart!
Carrie

But I will hope continually, and will yet praise thee more and more.

Psalm 71:14

TICK . . . TOCK

5/9/09

When . . . . did . . . . time . . . . stand . . . . still?

Sometimes I laugh when I think of the insane things that go through my head like, "3 1/2 weeks—that's not so long."

I AM happy to report that my week of medieval torture is behind me (chemos & transplant). Having all that culminate with the transplant was fitting. I think I told you that after they harvest your stem cells, they freeze them. When it comes time to put them back into your body, they have to go in FROZEN. Yeah, nothing like the feeling of "stem cell slushy" coursing through your veins. BURRRRRR!

Then you wait. My blood counts are pretty close to zero which is where they are supposed to be at this point. I think that's why I'm going a bit crazy—I now can not leave the confines of my air purified, germ free room. However, I CAN have visitors (as long as they're healthy). This is now Carrie eating her words of a month ago—"No need to visit. It's only 3 1/2 weeks. I'll be home before you know it!" I have since realized I have entered the land where a day is a month long and a month, a year. I know most of you live an hour (plus) away, but let me appeal to your curiosity—Is it Uncle Fester, a large egg or a turtle? (I've been called all three). I'm not vain—come see the turtle!!

If you can come, call my cell phone. If I sound desperate, well, there's no denying the obvious.

I DO realize there is no possible way I can thank you enough for getting me this far. I know I have some FIERCE prayer warriors out there.

Requests:

Cancer Free(dom)

That my blood cell counts come up with lightning speed, and I get out early for "good blood cell behavior".

That I don't get anymore negative side effects, and the one's I have go away.

Keep praying for J.T. and Max. I miss them enormously!!

I absolutely CHERISH you!! My most precious friends—here come the tears—I am overwhelmed by you!! God bless you and your families!!

Much Love,
Carrie

Then shall ye call upon me, and ye shall go and pray unto me, and I will hearken unto you.
And ye shall seek me, and find me, when ye shall search for me with all your heart.

Jeremiah 29: 12-13

THE COUNTDOWN

5/15/09

Hi Everyone!!

I'm counting down the days because it looks like I'll be going home MONDAY!!! Hallelujah! I've been feeling pretty good which is hard to do and remain in your hospital room!! Let me say—I would not be a sane human being if I didn't have you guys!! Your visits, your emails, your cards, your phone calls . . . . City of Hope would have taken me right from here to Happy Acres!! Hmmm, for all I know that is what is happening Monday.

Pray my blood counts continue to rise. My white blood cells are not where they should be yet, but my doctor is pretty confident that there will be plenty of them by Monday.

Another thing you have to accomplish before going home is getting your digestive system up and running again. I have been fed intravenously for about 10 days, and the stomach does NOT cooperate when you first put food in it again. So I am oh-so-slowly building up to the ultimate goal—a big, juicy hamburger!!

So those are my two big requests at this time—Blood & Food (EEK! Sounds like a vampire movie).

I thank the Lord upon every thought of you!

I Love You!!
Carrie

The Lord is my rock, and my fortress, and my deliverer; my God, my strength, in whom I will trust; my buckler, and the horn of my salvation, and my high tower.

Psalm 18:2

IT WAS THE DONKEY
AND THE CART

5/21/09

Hi Everyone!!

Okay, it was close to "straight jacket" time for Carrie those last days in the hospital. It is SOOOOOOO good to be home! I think it has taken me a while to write, because I just can't put into words how absolutely awful that experience was! No sugar coating that one! WHEW! Despite a few allergic reactions to the chemo, I had a picture perfect experience in the doctor's eyes. So we'll look through HER eyes and say "Thank you, Lord!!" We can look through my eyes and say, "Thank you, Lord, it's behind me!!" Again, I would not have made it through without you!!!

My blood counts are looking good. My prayer requests right now involve my favorite sport—eating! I can tell it's going to take quite a while to reach my ultimate goal of that hamburger. Please pray my digestive system and taste buds get back to normal soon. Granted, a little patience on my part wouldn't hurt!

I AM learning patience. This is going to be a slow recovery process. I guess it takes up to two years to get all your energy back, and I have a long list of things to avoid for 1 year. As long as I can do it at home—no problem!! Words can not EXPRESS how happy I am to be home!!

Hey, thank you again for everything!!!!! My prayers are with you, too!! I love you, dearly!! Did I mention I'm happy to be home?

Much Love,
Carrie

I will sing of the Lord's great love forever;
with my mouth I will make your faithfulness known
through all generations.

Psalm 89:1

GETTING BETTER (AGAIN)

5/30/09

I'm happy to report I DROVE today (first time in over a month). Max and I went to our favorite fast food place! It was so nice to be out of the house! I asked Max if we could take a drive to the beach to eat our tacos, but he just wanted to go home. Guess I'll have to take my "joy ride" later.

If I'm eating greasy tacos, my stomach MUST be doing pretty well! And it is! The nausea is gone—Thank heavens! And the digestive system is business as usual! Hey, I'm excited!! My taste buds are still not my own, but I'm sure that will come.

I have been extremely low on energy, but that has definitely improved the past couple of days! EVERYTHING is getting better with some things even back to normal!! How can I thank you, my dear prayer partners!!

Being held captive in my hospital room for three weeks has given me an empathy for prisoners. In fact, I've been reading Paul's (the apostle) letters that he wrote from prison with a whole new perspective. How could he write such beautiful letters to those churches when all I'd be thinking of is how to bust outta there? Seriously, I see a prison cell on my TV set, and I get the shivers.

I have my first follow-up doctor's visit Monday, and my first PET scan will be in about a month. I'm not hesitant to ask for your prayers—that the whole Carrie with cancer thing is over—oh, please Lord!

Hey, I won't be going many places this summer. I am giving you all an open invitation to come over and sit under an umbrella with me!

Much, Much Love,
Carrie

You will keep in perfect peace the mind that is dependent on You,
for it is trusting in You.
Trust in the Lord forever, because the Lord is an everlasting rock!

Isaiah 26:3-4

BREAKFAST ANYONE?

6/2/09

Hi Everyone!!

I just got back from my "joy ride". Ahh, to be among the crazy drivers of Orange County again! It's a beautiful thing!!

My doctor's appt. went well yesterday. I got the okay to eat whatever I want, so I am fully ready to have my old taste buds back!! Much to my surprise I threw up my breakfast before I left. My doctor says that happens all the time to people returning to the hospital. Our minds can be a scary thing!! (sorry, if that was TMI). My PET scan is on Friday, June 19. The last scan showed a small (non-cancerous) mass still in my chest. If it's still there, we're going to do radiation to zap it outta there!! So there's a prayer request—I would love for that thing to be gone! And, of course, for lymphoma to be gone forever . . . and ever . . . and ever!!

Well, I'm much balder than last year, and my hair shouldn't grow back for another couple months. Those of you in the hair ministry last year did such a good job, I'm putting in a prayer request with you. Shall we have a 5K?—We can call it "Carrie Kuliev's Run for the Hair".

I am really starting to feel human again!! It is SOOO
wonderful!

Much, Much Love,

Carrie

I will praise thee, O Lord, with my whole heart;
I will shew forth all thy marvelous works.
I will be glad and rejoice in thee:
I will sing praise to thy name, O thou most High.

Psalm 9:1-2

PET-SCAN-OPHOBIA

6/17/09

As some of you have surmised, Carrie is suffering from PET-scan-ophobia. Thankfully, I will be getting the results of my scan on the same day (Friday). None of that dreadful waiting!! YESSSSSS! I FEEL wonderful! I can't believe how much energy I have! I feel as well as I did last February—therein lies the "phobia". I AM trusting God! Eyes on Him—works every time!

Thank you for your prayers! Again, I am in disbelief at how great I feel! My current requests:

—No cancer

—No non-cancerous mass in my chest.

We'll find out Friday—I'll be sure to let you know!

Love and blessings,
Carrie

The Lord is with me; I will not be afraid.
What can man do to me?

Psalm 118:6

REMISSION—PART II

CARRIE WRITES A PSALM

6/19/09

Hi Everyone!!

Well, it's all GOOD NEWS!! Wohoo! I'll read the odd number verses while you, the congregation, read the even numbers: 1) The cancer is completely in remission 2) Lord, please let it stay that way forever 3) The non-cancerous mass has been a dead blob for over a year 4) Lord, please let it stay that way forever 5) Sooo no radiation for Carrie 6) Lord, please let it stay that way forever. I Carrieinthians 1: 1-6 (it's the "all about me" psalm). Anyway, I was dancing out of that hospital today!! Thank you, Lord!!!

One more small prayer request—the medication I take makes me nauseous, and I have to take it for 5 more months. It's crazy but the only time I don't feel nauseous is while I am eating and up to one hour after I have finished. So I basically spend most of my day thinking about what and when I'm going to eat next. You may have heard horrible rumors that this is nothing new in Carrie's life. Don't listen—this is an actual prayer request! Nausea is no laughing matter! Okay, I'm in a goofy mood, but seriously, any anti-nausea prayers you can throw my way are appreciated.

This morning at the hospital I felt as if a whole host of prayer warriors were with me and my parents. Can't thank you enough!

Much Love & Blessings,
Carrie

Praise the Lord! Praise the name of the Lord; praise Him, O you servants of the Lord.
Praise the Lord, for the Lord is good; make melody to His name, for it is sweet!

Psalm 135: 1 &3

WOLFMAN RETURNS!

6/24/09

Whoa, Partners, Whoa!! Good job with the hair growth prayers, but my hairs runneth over!! You're going to have to all buy me Norelco Shavers for Christmas!! I am FURRY—my face, my neck, my back!! It's the return of Wolfman (or should I say, Wolfwoman). I'm just thankful they're blond, or I'd be looking for a job in the circus by now. Just say NO to facial hair! The hair on my scalp is coming in nicely! It's about a quarter inch long, and very thick and silky. It is also a very nice, um . . . shall we say . . ."light black" color (yes, that would be gray).

If these are my biggest concerns, life must be pretty good. And it is!! I'm feeling great!! Lots of energy and minimal nausea—God is good, and is listening to your prayers!! I just got back from a trip to Yosemite with a good friend, and the boys and I are going to Washington D.C. in a couple of weeks! Can you believe it? Last May I couldn't even HOPE to be traveling this summer. I'm just happy to be able to drive to the grocery store, so as you can imagine, I'm walking around in a perpetually happy state! Hair . . . Shmair! I'm embracing the wolfwoman inside me!

J.T. and Max are doing well. I sure have enjoyed every minute we've had together this summer!! This Washington D.C. trip is the first one the boys and I will be taking—just the three of us. Any and all prayers for our travels (8/17-8/23) are appreciated!! Thank you so much for your prayers for my family!!

Much, Much Love,
Carrie

My favorite time of day in Yosemite is in the evening when the entire valley and cliffs are shrouded in shadow except for Half Dome, which is the last thing in Yosemite Valley to catch the light of the setting sun. I look at it and see God's creativity in His creation. His attention to detail always fascinates me, but this one—I don't see how anyone can ignore the Creator!

From the rising of the sun to the place where it sets,
the name of the Lord is to be praised.

Psalm 113:3

FEELING PRETTY GREAT!

8/26/09

Hi Everyone!!

Well, a million thank you's for your prayers for my vacation with J.T. and Max! It went swimmingly!! When my boys were little, they used to hold my hand for safety. Now I hold the hands of my (almost 6 foot tall) boys for **my** safety!! We all enjoyed D.C.!! I fell in love again with the Smithsonian Museums. I especially appreciated that I could walk quite a bit before my feet started killing me, and my energy level never dropped! The Lord clearly went ahead of us each day providing many miracles. It was great!!

I had a "check up on Carrie's blood" appointment with Dr. Big Cheese at City of Hope on Monday. Some of my blood counts have dipped—not a great thing—both my white and red blood cells included. So my newest prayer request would be that my bone marrow would kick into gear and produce more blood cells. Also, my short term memory loss has bumped itself up to a whole new level. Please pray this chemo side effect goes away before I become like Dori from "Finding Nemo"—though I do like her mantra "Just keep swimming—just keep swimming".

An anecdote—that stem cell transplant that I had in May—it feels like it was years ago—maybe memory loss isn't such a bad thing!! I sure love you guys!! You are in my thoughts and prayers!! Keep pedaling—the road can be rough—I'm glad I'm not driving!!

God bless you, precious prayer partners!!

Much Love,
Carrie

Trust in the Lord forever.
For in God the Lord, we have an everlasting Rock.

Isaiah 26:4

HERE'S TO THE DAY-TO-DAY

9/26/09

Hi Everyone!!

Life is HOPPING! Going to the grocery store, visiting the gas station, driving on the FREEWAY! Having renewed energy and a new appreciation of life (again) sure puts a different spin on things. It does NOT get old! I'm hoping it hangs on for quite a while!! I enjoy mundane events and the time that I get to spend with my family and friends is an incredible treat!!

I had my appointment with my local oncologist a few days ago. He burst in the room with, "Here's our success story!" It felt so wonderful to hear that—I wanted to stand up and say, "I'd like to thank the academy of medical sciences, the Lord, my mother and father, and most importantly, my incredible prayer partners for their perseverance and swollen knees!"

Really, you guys, I am sooo thankful for you!! I feel great!! My blood counts are going up! Yay! J.T. and Max are doing well! We're all settling into the new school year.

I love you and thank the Lord everyday for you!

Much Love & Blessings,
Carrie

Sing to the Lord with thanksgiving;
Sing praises to our God on the lyre.

Psalms 147:7

A HUG FROM AN ANGEL

2/25/11

Well, Carrie got an enormous "God Hug" today. A friend and I were having a nice afternoon running errands together when she got a phone call. A friend of hers asked if she could pick up her children from school, because she was sick. So off we went to the middle school, and soon one of her daughters got in the car.

"Hi, I'm Carrie," I said to her.

"Are you the Carrie with cancer?" she asked enthusiastically.

"Well, I guess that would be me."

"I've been praying for you for the last three years!"

I was speechless.

Our whole youth group is praying for you!"

Oh my! I was overwhelmed and humbled!

I WAS so excited to show her how healthy I was and how long my hair had gotten, and to let her know God truly is answering her prayers!

Wow!! I'm still pretty speechless. Thank you, Lord! And thank you prayer partners (wherever you may be)! I'm praying for you!

Love you truly,
Carrie

The eternal God is thy refuge, and underneath are the everlasting arms.

Deuteronomy 33:27

CONCLUSION

4/8/11

Well, everyone, I am coming up on my two year anniversary of my stem cell transplant. They weren't kidding about that two year estimate of getting my energy back. I've had weeks where I am running circles around my kids, and weeks where I have thought of starting a ministry called SFG—Slugs for God. Our motto can be "I can do ALL things through Christ who strengthens me." Philippians 4:13. However, I have definitely noticed that I am almost fully back to my old trouble-making self!! So far my PET scans have been clear of cancer. Thanks be to God and my knee callused prayer partners!

During my two years of fighting this disease, I received many a comment from people amazed at how upbeat I could remain, and concerned that I didn't really know what I was facing. That, my friends, is the beauty of knowing, trusting and believing in God. We can look cancer, even death, in the face and have peace. God is in the valleys of life as well as the mountain tops. Sometimes it takes the valleys of life for us to stop and hear His voice more clearly. Each verse on these pages was a gift of the Lord to me. Drink them in!

Life is short! It's but a breath! Seek God and look up—heaven is but a breath away! And **that** is a beautiful thing!!